T0417824

THE ENVIRONMENT

Written by
William Anthony

Designed by
Danielle Rippengill

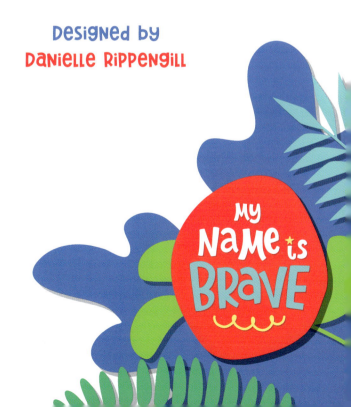

My Name is BRAVE

Library of Congress Control Number:
2024945365

ISBN
979-8-89359-259-7 (library bound)
979-8-89359-267-2 (paperback)
979-8-89359-282-5 (epub)
979-8-89359-275-7 (hosted ebook)

Printed in the United States of America
Mankato, MN
012025

Written by:
William Anthony

Edited by:
Robin Twiddy

Designed by:
Danielle Rippengill

Image Credits

All images are courtesy of Shutterstock.com, unless otherwise specified. With thanks to Getty Images, Thinkstock Photo
and iStockphoto. Cover – Svetlosila, Zenstockers, rosewind, ursulamea, GoodStudio. Images used on every page – Svetlosila,
rosewind, ursulamea. 2 – GoodStudio. 4&5 – Anatoliy Karlyuk, Halfpoint, M_Agency, SeventyFour. 6&7 – Lakkana Boonrat,
NadyGinzburg, PARALAXIS, Patrick Foto. 8&9 – Antonello Marangi, Daniele COSSU, dominika zara, GoodStudio. 10&11 –
DisobeyArt, Halfpoint, wavebreakmedia, GoodStudio. 12&13 – John Cairns, CC BY 4.0 <https://creativecommons.org/licenses/
by/4.0>, via Wikimedia Commons, Ben Warwick-Champion, Ron Adar, GoodStudio. 14&15 – fizkes, Joe Ferrer, wavebreakmedia,
GoodStudio. 16&17 – Dennis Wegewijs, Fabian Plock, Joseph Sohm, By The-time-line - Own work, CC BY-SA 3.0, GoodStudio.
18&19 – Rawpixel.com, Rupert Rivett, Syda Productions, GoodStudio. 20&21 – Boxed Lunch Production, soft_light, tonyzhao120,
GoodStudio. 22&23 – KlingSup, Lemon Tree Images, Syda Productions, GoodStudio. 24&25 – StudioSmart,
wavebreakmedia, Greenbangalore, CC BY-SA 4.0 <https://creativecommons.org/licenses/by-sa/4.0>,
via Wikimedia Commons, GoodStudio. 26&27 – Ellyy, Hajakely, Stock-Asso, GoodStudio.
28&29 – 24K-Production, POP-THAILAND, GoodStudio.

CONTENTS

WORDS THAT LOOK LIKE this ARE EXPLAINED IN THE GLOSSARY ON PAGE 30.

BEING BRAVE

What makes someone brave? Does it mean not being afraid of things? Is it when you don't hide behind a pillow when you watch a scary movie? Is it when you are not scared to go down a humongous water slide? **NO!**

WHEN WAS THE LAST TIME YOU DID SOMETHING BRAVE?

Being brave is about being frightened to do something, but still doing it because you know you need to. It is about standing up for things or people even when you are nervous or scared.

Activism

It can be quite scary to make big changes in the world. Some people might disagree with what you say. Other people might try to stop you. Activists are people who stand up bravely against things they think are bad. They believe they are trying to change the world for the better.

Causing Change

Activism can happen in lots of different ways. Many activists will take part in protests. Others might perform speeches to lots of people. In today's world, lots of activists try to spread their ideas on the internet and **social media**.

THE ENVIRONMENT

Head outside. Are you there? Great! Now, take a look around you. Look at the bushes and trees, the roads and sidewalks, and the animals on the ground and in the air. All of these things make up the environment.

WHAT CAN YOU SEE OUTSIDE?

The environment needs help. We must look after it because, for a very long time, humans have not. Many people still do not look after the planet today.

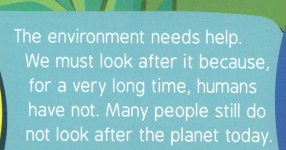

Humans have been careless in looking after the planet. Climate change is one of the biggest **threats** our planet faces. Climate change is when the planet slowly gets hotter over a long time. Burning things such as coal, oil, and gas speeds up climate change. That means many of our cars, buses, and planes are making things worse. The same goes for some of the ways we make electricity.

THIS IS WHY LOTS OF ACTIVISTS ARE TRYING TO CHANGE THE WAY WE TREAT THE ENVIRONMENT!

Some people also cut down trees. Trees help to slow down climate change and are homes for many animals. Some animals have gone **extinct** because of humans hurting them or destroying their homes.

GRETA THUNBERG

Greta Thunberg is best known for challenging world leaders over climate change. When she was 15 years old, she protested outside of the Swedish Parliament. She carried a sign that read "School Strike for Climate." Soon, students across the world had joined Greta and were on **strike** from school to protest.

SKOLSTR
FÖR
KLIMA

GRETA STARTED A <u>movement</u> CALLED FRIDAYS FOR FUTURE, ALSO KNOWN AS SCHOOL STRIKE FOR CLIMATE.

Greta sailed to New York to attend a **United Nations** climate conference. There, she gave a speech that was impossible to ignore.

"YOU ALL COME TO US YOUNG PEOPLE FOR HOPE. HOW DARE YOU! YOU HAVE STOLEN MY DREAMS AND MY CHILDHOOD WITH YOUR EMPTY WORDS!"

Greta has become a **symbol** for young climate activists, and her passion and bravery have inspired a whole generation of young environmentalists.

SKOLSTREJK FOR KLIMATET

READ PAGE 10 TO FIND OUT MORE ABOUT PROTESTS!

PROTESTING FOR CHANGE

WE NEED A CHANGE

So, what exactly is a protest? You may have seen one in a city or town center before. A protest is usually an event where a group of people who disagree with something gather together to demand change.

Many protests happen in places where important decisions are made, such as in front of a **government** building. People might make signs or shout **chants** together.

Make a Sign

Signs are a very useful way of getting a message across. Why not try making one yourself? Let's take a look at what to do.

ONE

Grab yourself some cardboard for your sign. Cardboard can be **recycled** when we are done!

TWO

Find some markers, crayons, or paint to write your message.

THREE

Think about what you would like to say. What would you like to be changed? Your message needs to be short, but powerful enough to make people listen.

FOUR

Write your message on your sign! Maybe you could draw a picture to go with it.

CLIMATE CHANGES, WHY CAN'T WE?

— DAVID —
ATTENBOROUGH

Have you have ever watched a TV show about **nature**? Then there is a big chance you have heard David Attenborough's voice! David is a very famous person when it comes to talking about the environment.

David started making TV shows about our planet and its animals all the way back in 1954. Since then, he has become the voice of some of the biggest nature programs in the world.

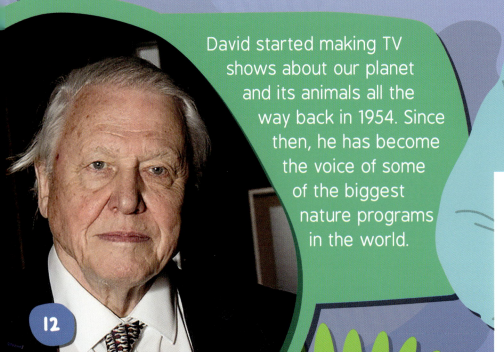

David Attenborough has traveled around the world to make speeches to important leaders about stopping climate change. He has spoken at United Nations Climate Change events, for wildlife charities, and at lots of universities.

"A crime has been committed, and ... I'm of such an age that I was able to see it beginning."

Because David is so famous, he could lose a lot by making these speeches about climate change if people disagree with him. However, David has been brave and used his fame to make a big impact on the world and climate change.

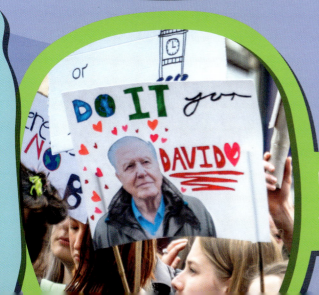

DAVID HAS INSPIRED LOTS OF YOUNG PEOPLE TO BE BRAVE, TOO.

MAKING A SPEECH

David Attenborough has become well known for his speeches on climate change and the environment. A speech is a long talk someone gives to a group of people, called an audience.

Speeches are a good way of getting an important message across to people. Speeches can last for minutes or even hours. Standing up in front of lots of people and talking can be frightening, but anyone can do it if they are brave!

Get Writing

Are you feeling brave enough to make a speech about the planet? Let's start writing one!

ONE

The best way to prepare a speech is to write it down. Use a computer to type it out, or a paper and pencil instead.

THREE

Try reading all of your ideas out loud. Practice, practice, and practice again!

TWO

Think about what you want to say. Write each idea down. When you have all your ideas, try putting them into an order that makes sense.

FOUR

Now that your speech is ready, you could perform it to your grown-ups at home, your class, or your friends.

IDEAS

WANGARI MAATHAI

Being brave can sometimes be about doing what you think is right, even though you know that you will have to face **consequences**. Wangari Maathai was from Kenya, in Africa. Wangari was known for her bravery in trying to protect the environment.

In 1977, Wangari founded the Green Belt Movement in Kenya. This was all about getting people to plant trees. Most of these people were women. Planting trees helps the environment a lo Many people call plants the **lungs** of the planet.

THESE TREES ARE READY TO BE PLANTED.

One of the bravest things Wangari Maathai did was take on Kenya's president. The president of Kenya is the person in charge of the country. Kenya's president wanted to chop down huge forests of trees to build **luxury** houses.

Wangari had been put in prison many times for standing up to people who are in charge. However, that didn't stop her. In 1998, she stopped the president's plans and saved the forest. Then, in 2002, she was chosen to be part of the Kenyan government!

CUTTING DOWN TREES IN FORESTS IS CALLED DEFORESTATION.

NOT MANY PEOPLE ARE BRAVE ENOUGH TO TAKE ON THEIR COUNTRY'S LEADER. WANGARI WAS!

17

LEADING BY EXAMPLE

It is easy to tell someone to do something. However, it doesn't mean they will do it. Sometimes, in order to get people to want to help you, you need to inspire them by being a role model. A role model is someone that other people want to be like.

Wangari Maathai was a role model for lots of people. Rather than just tell people that they should protest or make a change, she took matters into her own hands to save the environment.

Start to Plant

Wangari was famous for her Green Belt Movement. It involved lots of people planting trees. Trees and other plants take **carbon dioxide** out of the air. So, the more plants, the better!

ONE

Let's grow some plants to help the environment! Use flower seeds, or plant a small tree like Wangari did.

TWO

Dig a small hole in some soil outside where there is lots of light. Put in the seeds or small tree. Fill the hole in with soil.

FOUR

Water your plants often, and watch them grow!

THREE

Plants need water. Carefully pour some water over the soil.

HANS COSMAS NGOTEYA

What job would you like when you grow up? Choosing a job can be difficult. Hans Cosmas Ngoteya wanted to be a park ranger in Tanzania, which is a country in Africa. It was a good job, and he would get to photograph and film animals, which he loved doing.

A PARK RANGER LOOKS AFTER WILDLIFE IN A PARTICULAR PARK.

PARK RANGER

However, Hans saw a better way to protect wildlife and the environment. It meant that he had to go for a less **secure** job that he couldn't be sure would succeed. It was a very brave thing to do.

20

Hans started a charity called the Landscape and Conservation Mentors Organization. It aims to teach people how to live together with wildlife safely, so that no animals get hurt and the environment doesn't get damaged.

Hans believes that it is everyone's job to look after the environment and protect all the animals and plants within it.

SETTING UP A CHARITY

Helping others is a wonderful way to make the world a better place for everyone to live. Charities help people all over the world who need **support**.

Some charities might work to help people who don't have enough food or a place to live. Other charities, such as the one Hans Cosmas Ngoteya started, help keep animals safe. People can give money to these charities so they can carry out their work. This is called donating.

First Steps

What is important to you about the environment? Is there anything that you think needs to change to protect it? Let's use that idea and pretend to set up a charity! Here's what you'll need:

ONE

Charity Name: You'll need to think of a name for your charity. It will need to be memorable!

TWO

Logo: Your charity will need a logo that people can recognize right away!

FOUR

Events: You'll need lots of events to raise money. What sorts of events will your charity organize?

THREE

Mission Statement: A mission statement is what problem your charity wants to solve, who they want to help, and how they want to do it.

MALAIKA VAZ

One of the most important ways to protect the environment is by teaching other people. This is called education. Educating people about problems with the environment, as well as how to solve them, will help our planet for years to come.

Malaika Vaz is a famous filmmaker. She makes programs about animals and the environment. Malaika has put herself in dangerous situations to help educate people.

THAT DOESN'T MEAN YOU SHOULD PUT YOURSELF IN DANGEROUS SITUATIONS, THOUGH!

Malaika has filmed a program about the illegal trafficking of manta rays. Illegal trafficking is when people buy, sell, and move people or animals around the world when it is against the **law**. Some people do this to use the body parts of the animals for different things.

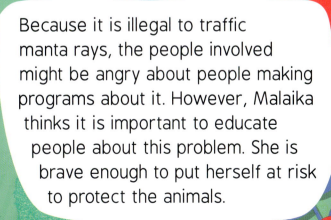

MANTA RAY

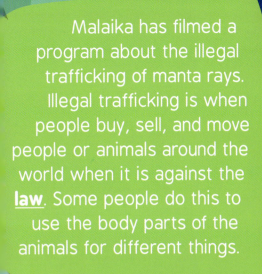

Because it is illegal to traffic manta rays, the people involved might be angry about people making programs about it. However, Malaika thinks it is important to educate people about this problem. She is brave enough to put herself at risk to protect the animals.

RAISING AWARENESS

TV shows that **investigate** things in real life are called documentaries. They are a very important way that we can educate one another about the world.

Both Malaika Vaz and David Attenborough make documentaries about animals and the environment. For a long time, documentaries mostly showed us the good and exciting parts about our planet. Today, documentaries often show us about the problems the environment is facing.

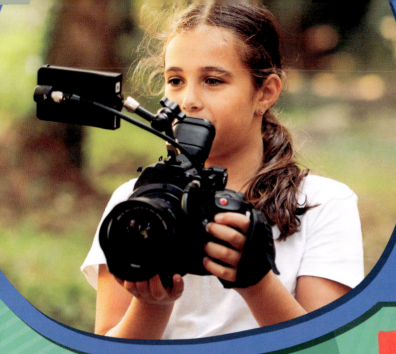

Start Filming

If you could educate people about the problems the environment is facing, what would you teach them? Let's make a documentary about it! All you need is a phone camera.

One

Decide on your topic before you film anything. What message do you want to get across?

Two

Research your topic. It is important to put lots of facts into your documentary.

Four

Record your documentary!

Three

Find a good place to film. Make sure it is somewhere safe. An adult can help film you by holding the phone.

MY NAME IS BRAVE

There are lots of people out there in the world who are trying to help change things for the better. You don't need to be famous like the people in this book. You just need to believe that you can make a difference.

Making a change that protects or helps the environment can be scary. Some people will not like what you say, and they'll disagree with you. Others might try to make it hard for you to make the positive changes you believe in.

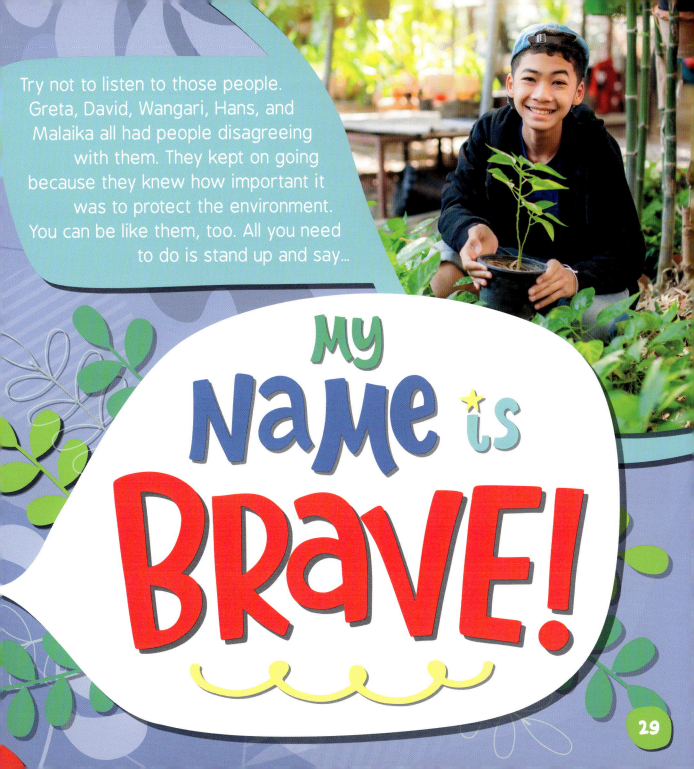

Try not to listen to those people. Greta, David, Wangari, Hans, and Malaika all had people disagreeing with them. They kept on going because they knew how important it was to protect the environment. You can be like them, too. All you need to do is stand up and say...

My Name is Brave!

GLOSSARY

carbon dioxide a gas that can cause problems for the planet when there is too much of it

chants words or phrases that a person or group repeats over and over again

consequences things that happen as a result of someone's actions

extinct no longer existing in the world

government the group of people who control and make decisions for a country

investigate to try to find out the facts about something in order to learn about it

law a rule that people in a particular place must live by

lungs the parts of the body that people and animals use to breathe

luxury very expensive and having a very high quality

movement when many people work together to do or achieve something

nature all the things in the world that were not made by humans

recycled made into something new

secure safe and not needing to be worried about

social media websites and apps on which people can create online accounts and communities where they can share information or messages

strike an event when a group of people stop doing their work in order to force others to agree to what they are asking for

support help that is given in the form of money or other needed things

symbol something or someone that represents something else

threats people or things that could cause harm or damage

United Nations a worldwide organization that most countries belong to, in which those countries can discuss important things and make plans

INDEX

CLIMATE CHANGES, WHY CAN'T WE?